JN411156

Beginning the End

Beginning the End

A collection of new poems by Kim Keun
Translated by Deborah Kim

K POET

아시아

Contents

BEGINNING THE END

Prologue

One day a beast arrived
It walked through the alley
with languid strides and
climbed over the wall with
its long arms It strode up
the steps and opened my
bedroom door It walked as
though through water its long
fur undulating It approached
me slowly yet a strand of hair
swayed slowly remaining at
each place it passed As if
there was a line of identical

beasts following the movements
of the first beast like they were
approaching me Time stretched
on endlessly each movement
divided unable to go on stalled
only traces of the beast seemed
to be moving I guessed that they
could be found at each turn of
slowed time I couldn't be sure
but the beast resembled an
orangutan It came to me
gibbering human speech But
I couldn't understand a word
The beast couldn't relieve its

tedium in the wind called forth
by its waving arm traces of its
hair were strewn through my
room Even after stirring up
chaos and hair the beast
couldn't relieve its tedium it
turned and as it walked out
the beast paused at my door
and turned its head and
called my name yet again I
couldn't understand it
The beast went back the way it
came each place it had passed
beasts were fixed in place coming

and going at once briefly blurring
boundaries I could sense that the
traces would scatter in the air
I hurried to piece together
the words that had been left
behind trying this way and that
way to piece them together like
a puzzle Finally a semblance
of a sentence but the words were
the same as something I had
scribbled long ago in my journal
my body trembled at the
inexplicability of it all I couldn't
even dare to guess my own name

I think I've heard of orangutan hair

being used to make brushes

but never heard of the brushes

being used to write It would have

been nice to make brushes out

of the beast's hair but all traces

of the beast were gone Vanished

as though they had never existed

Part 1

Chapter 1

A Thing wakes in dark Feathers made of darkness tickles the Thing The Thing squirms Soft noises sound from the floor arrhythmic Of something falling Trying to heave itself up and soon falling back down The sound repeated and repeated At last the sound of a sigh seeped out in the darkness but couldn't break the dark's desolation The lump behind the faint dark sigh Its silence can't cut through the uncuttable disappearing darkness doesn't waver doesn't soar Even if we say the darkness is just darkness the Thing will wake

Just the fact of its consciousness makes

me speak In-between waking and slumber

in-between silence and speech I say It is

just a Thing undefined formless Merely the

narrative of its awakening is happening As

the event of its awakening emerges I begin

to speak and as soon as the beginning begins

It becomes the Thing though it is unseeable

It squirms in the darkness signals that It is

alive and breathing Was it the start of life

or the end or was it hopeless progression I

couldn't tell It was in the darkness and I

too was in the darkness

The Thing doesn't know if it has a head or eyes It may have opened its eyes It may be blinking Even if it flutters its eyelids once the Thing opens its eyes the darkness will permeate its pupils like a shadow eaten up by darkness Its nostrils may flare sniffsniffsniff The Thing might be assessing the darkness The stiff joints of its arms and legs don't move smoothly It might be floundering It might be naked The Thing might be sweeping across the floor with its naked body wriggling from place to place

Words sink down like heavy smoke Unable to reach it It is simply it I am simply I and theory is simply theory And I am always lingering before theory The present is forever post-theory paused and never takes place Even if I develop it within theory seldom does it progress I face the pre-development hesitant unsure of what to do with it but I speak and the fact of its existence doesn't change And all I can do is try to push it force it into theory

Let's say the Thing is a person lying in

the darkness That the Thing was lying
down and trying to stand Let's say the
Thing failed that it repeated its failure
Let's say the Thing let out a sigh after
failing that it continued trying and
failing trying and failing Let's say the
Thing opened its eyes Let's say the
Thing could see nothing that it could
only tell its eyes were open or closed
by the sensation in its eyelids Let's say
the Thing tried to move its arms its legs
slightly That its arms and legs moved
stiffly as though its limbs are not its
own like they're moving on their own that

their eyes nose mouth are gathered in the
center of its face that its using all its
strength That its blood is flowing bit by
bit in its limbs at long last its limbs feel
like its own though they aren't moving
perfectly yet bit by bit gradually step
by step they're moving finally its fingertips

How far can words move Words can't be
unraveled they hesitate and linger how
deeply can they stagnate Now words
have no past no future only the present
Words leave me endlessly in the present
Nonsense grows thick as its branches

stretch out it becomes difficult to tell the non from the sense Day from night If it's the breaking light of dawn or the fading glow of evening It's difficult to discern the non from the sense after all non is non Sense is sense Gibberish lays eggs here and hatches them The children of Gibberish are myriad They cover this place They sink down like heavy smoke that can't touch you You're still waking and I am only speaking

The Thing is waking in the darkness It wakes slowly raises its body up Lifts its

head and looks around There's only
darkness only silence It feels around
Starting from the floor passing over
toes calves thighs slowly carefully as
though it's counting each hair its
fingertips take in stomach and chest
and arms and neck Its body is warm
and soft it is not yet cold not yet hard
The Thing can feel that it is not yet
cold or hard—its fingertips feel and
it's like touching a stranger's flesh
its identity is not easily revealable
is not easily determinable Within
the darkness of words within the

dark feathers of words the Thing
is touching its body like a stranger's

Words aren't clear Its direction isn't
distinct The Thing isn't clear and I
too am not clear It appeared within
words it is just starting to movc I
am hiding that I too just appeared
I am hiding behind the time of
words that aren't coming

Chapter 2

Hey! Is there anyone out there? Is it just me here Just a body I guess you could say is me Half-sitting up fingertips barely extended Just patpatpat sweeping darkness Just touchtouch feeling dark flesh Hey! If you can feel my presence Answer me Even if they're not words but mere sounds If I say hey at least say ho Can't you do that much Anyway until I can speak I'll keep trickling sound that's my plan until someone gets here Hey! Is anyone out there? I'm certain something happened here I'm certain someone abandoned me here If not how could I be

lying here stripped down If not why would
I be here like a newborn gauging the
darkness in this darkness unable to speak
just gibbering away If not otherwise
how could my memory be so pitch-black
Hey! Anyone out there Answer me

I think I have heard of darkness being
like feathers but without having heard
so much as a crow's caw there's no way
darkness is feathers This darkness that
shrouds me is like gloopy mud My body
is being molded within that mud
wherever I touch it is being made into

existence Isn't it obvious there's
nothing but darkness here I must feel
to know what's there It's how I learned
the truth of my nakedness I'm saying I
haven't heard a crow caw even once
nothing altogether silence altogether
Anyway I'm saying in that pitch black
darkness there's something there I can't
see My body hasn't stuck itself together
yet Something is lurking what signs do
I have to send out for them to come?
Once they come will they stick to me
will they stick? Will they make it so I
can recognize myself? I'm saying right

now I can't recognize me so why am
I calling myself me when I can't see

Even when difficulty adds upon difficulty
it still wouldn't be as difficult as me Sigh
It's really not here Okay can't feel my head
Okay my fingertips pass my Adam's apple
but my fingertips can't glide to the curve
of my chin they stop in mid-air and may
not rebound Unsure of where to go my
fingertips are being abandoned in the
empty darkness it's not just my fingertips
being abandoned As the truth of my
headlessness emerges my arms legs

writhe flounder wriggle Like a rag doll's
shaking my body shakes aimlessly Like a
chicken with its head cut off going off going
crazy throwing a fit going wild—It's all just
my imagination My body's weak drooping
arms and legs plop back down to the
ground sprawl out I want to blame my
arms and legs for not moving properly
but then my head Where is it? Is it
opening and closing its eyes somewhere
I'm sure it's dark there too—no my head
might be here and my body over there
Anyway whether it's here or there it's all
dark right it's all dark Yes it's all dark yes

yesyes yes and that's why I'm here

What is happening what is going
on What isn't happening what isn't
going on What's left is a body what's
gone is an entire head or it could be
the opposite A sound on the verge of
escaping just barely stopped by the
neck left atop this body Is sound seeping
out the hole punched out the neck or in
some unknown place is there a head a
tongue growing stiff sound trickling
between the lips? Or if not that
are words seeping out from the body

or the head or unable to spill out circling
inside futilely? Where is the interior of
words where is the exterior? Is the head's
exterior the body Outside the body is the
head just rolling around Who is asking
these questions is it the body or the head?
Who can make these questions stop? I
may or may not have been stuck in the
bowels of darkness in the darkness to be
eaten up by darkness for good I may be
rotting Rotting with flesh maybe melting
away Turning black Purge fluid may be
flowing the odor may be foul The head
and the body may bet on the street who

will rot first I might bet the two can't
face each other I don't know that I don't
know I may not know that I do not know

Chapter 3

As I wrote ***Beginning the End*** the sunlight began to wane The sunlight gnawed away all day at the letters on the old bookshelf The sunlight that had been preying on the letters retreated The shards of words leftover were swept into the room corners Darkness roosts The leftover words may become Darkness' quarry I write ***Beginning the End*** The sunlight fades me Darkness wears me out ***Beginning the End*** It's as though I've written this all my life Not begin at the end not begin after the end not ending the end not beginning the

beginning not even ending the beginning
Beyond faded and worn splintering
crumbling right before it disappears
completely ***End the Beginning***

I wanted to write Even as I saw myself
Beginning the End Here all the trees
have a touch of the carnivorous about
them A nonexistent mother keeps getting
up ***Beginning the End*** A swamp where
a young child drowned appears The trees
have no mouths only teeth No not teeth
only the memory of teeth Not the traces
of lost teeth Languid flesh ripped torn

and torn apart The wind scattered I want
to hang on the wood bark and write
Beginning the End I wanted to write
Even as I saw myself It seems a long time
ago and recently A swamp where a young
child drowned grows lush from somewhere
The sounds of eating devouring annihilation
and creation A silent mother Countless
mothers who don't exist keep getting up Get
up and beat me endlessly I wanted to write
Even as I saw myself ***Beginning the End***
The forest swells with needle teeth I see all
the trees here have a trace of the carnivorous
I wanted to write I couldn't find a single well

I couldn't find a single species on the ground
Lying on the ground blood flows from the ears
above that flesh a face sprouts Faces they come
into existence and destruct I wanted to write
Even as I saw myself ***Beginning the End*** the
shadows shake horribly they only shake at the
things not there shaking each others' bodies
Beginning the End mixing and mixing
abandoning a nonexistent mother gets up
lost ***Beginning the End*** conceals one eye
A child who doesn't know who they are
Beginning the End sees the swamp they
drowned in I wanted to write Trees hang
from the air they slip slipping falling

Beginning the End neck I wanted to

write Even as I saw myself In my dreams

I hung ***the end*** beyond dreams I hung

beginning not a single well was to be

found here trees have a trace of the

carnivorous ***the end beginning*** a

long time ago It felt like ***the end*** the

beginning feels like just a moment ago

I ***begin*** seeing ***in*** me ***the*** writing ***end***

I wanted to

though I wanted to

Beginning the End sticks to me like

Spanish needles Knee-high grass meets
a deep black forest I don't know if the
trail is faltering or not at what point I
may be buried where it's stuck it clings
squeezes between layers of clothes
pierces piercingly stings Shaking and
shaking all of no use no matter how
you try it can't be detached it's
tenacious ***Beginning the End***

because of it
because because It's only because

Writing ***Beginning the End*** inevitably

Beginning the End now in a room that's wearing down the black of my body tends to leak into darkness Black stains litter my body like an empty ink bottle Writing ***Beginning the End*** however the darkness doesn't start from the outside wouldn't it have come from the inside? Despite suspicions The crumbs of words the sunlight left behind the consonants and vowels are already separate can't be told apart If they permeate darkness perhaps sunlight doesn't begin from outside but spills out from within If so could you call it a hint and premonition Even if you call it a dark hint a dazzling premonition ***Beginning the***

End even if it's a dazzling hint and a dark
premonition fading wearing down Writing
Beginning the End this way and that way
My body has nothing not even words left
nothing apart from ***Beginning the End***
absolutely nothing just an achingly hollow
stained wrung out few drops of darkness
left to write ***Beginning the End*** Whether
to live in a hint or die in a premonition
hoping this way or that way now or then
with only rotting time left Barely

only
truly only

writing

Beginning the End

Part 2

Chapter 1

I will call the Thing "You" you are

human because you are presumed

human you need a personal pronoun

The first person doesn't fit we need a

delineation between you and me

Without that you will flounder about

in my memory The third person isn't

right it'd be trouble if you're too

distant from me If I call you by the

third person there's no you but another

name altogether that comes between

you and me When I don't call you "you"

I won't know where I am When I call

you "you" it feels like I'm giving you

orders without anyone's interference

and you'll be here I'll get to see you here

You move all around You grow brighter

vaguely Faint light draws boundaries on

your body You have no head You cannot

see You move a little You spread out your

arms You grope the floor You focus on

the feeling in your fingertips You crawl

forward as far as your arms can reach

You spread your arms out again focus on

the feeling in your fingertips You move

again You have no head your body is

bewildered at times falling down You get

up again dragging your knee one hand
leans on the floor You stretch out the
other arm as far as you can spread out
your fingers as wide as you can focus on
each nerve in the fingers your hands
touch nothing your knees akimbo you
pull onc thigh up towards your body
moves forward your knee pit folds out
at an obtuse angle from your backside
This time it's the other arm outstretched
the other hand waves Again you keep
moving nothing can be felt it's all
emptiness you move again your body's
boundaries stain light only the light of the

hollow above your shoulders grows sharper

I had to get rid of your head I needed
light to see you be it faint It wasn't enough
to pluck out your eyeballs it's not merely
sight I ought to deprive you of time to even
think I don't care where your head was
dumped whether it's opening or closing
its eyes if it's still bleeding if you can see
me and think about me that's not complete
oppression I will oppress you I will oppress
you By chance if a light appears don't
mistake it as a place for you Without
memory how can a place come into being

You're a moving body A lump of flesh with movement enough That is enough Enough

As you go along your hand touches something You stop—you don't go further you touch a hard surface rough and bumpy A skinny cylinder stretches out vertically You presume it must be a tree You touch the tree You grab the tree with both hands You raise one knee push against the tree and lift yourself up with the force You tense your raised knee and sole of your foot You slowly rise as you stretch your hands out a little higher You explore the bark of the tree You stand up fully You feel a knotted rope around the tree level with your chest your hands stop moving higher You follow the rope you extend your hands follow the rope gropinggroping you follow your hands you turn your body along the way your hand feels something you stop You recoil in haste your body freezes for a moment Your face doesn't contort in shock You have no head you cannot see Your fingertips tremble carefully reach towards it Your fingertips detect that it's tied to the tree slowly You touch it you can sense its softness your fingertips can feel its warmth can feel it is gradually growing cooler Your fingers can

sense it's a body it's human Both your hands
touch starting from the toes to the ankles past
the calves over the knees over the thighs past
the groin over the navel past the pit of the
stomach over angular ribs over the chest past
the shoulders over the collarbone past the
Adam's apple—gropinggroping—the chin—
touchingtouching touchingtouching your
hands can't go any further Bewildered
your hands lose their way

I should stop speaking The words that
bound you grab me by the throat From
my constricted throat words seep out like

air from a deflating balloon and suffocate

me Now within words that sound like the

crying of a bird your body feels but

emotions are only movement I should

stop with this body before words'

emotions spread to me like a contagion

before I reflect on this nonsense's

nonsense-ness Before that I must infect

you with my strangling words To you

your words may have existed but in my

words your words weren't there—Words?

From a headless body? I couldn't even

imagine it When you began to move in

fact I was suffocating Was it only my

pointed words for you that strangled

me or you moving within my words

Have your words escaped from within

mine or is it that I must live on to see

I'm suffocating Suffocate but I'm not

sad—sad I'm not sad I'm not suffocating

Chapter 2

You have a head and you're tied up

I'm not tied up but I don't have a head

Everyone has one

Everyone is missing one

Everyone has been tied up once

Everyone has been sprawled out

*

My headless words Do they have sound if

they don't my words may be flowing out

like rants and raves from a neck that is

nothing more than a stump The sounds
leaking from that neck hole are irrelevant
to my words It's only right to divide words
and sounds Words are words sounds are
sounds Are soundless words even speech?
Can you call words un-enunciated words?
Let's say they're words Even if you had ears
you could never hear me My words in the
end become impossible they are noises that
couldn't become words so my gibberish was
wrong Would it be right to say that they
were words that couldn't reach sound You
may wonder why next to a bound you there's
a headless body occasionally hiss-hissing

leaking air splayed out You may slip words

through your tender lips You have no ears

you cannot hear me From the start we

couldn't get on speaking terms no matter

how you look at it you couldn't listen or

speak Wholly speechless ranting things

we're unable to hear we are just here even

if we're not here we may just be here Sigh

even if we're not here we are here

*

If only a breeze would blow from

somewhere Not the air seeping

out from the body Not a sharp
thin wind rising up like anxious
eyes hiding in an alley or some
other corner crouching and
trembling Rather a bracing wind
from a distant mountain range
splintered by the pine forest that
strikes the arms Reaching the
bamboo grove makes the entire
grove shiver and shimmer If the
wind blew in it would be vivid
Yours and mine this flesh warm
blood should be flowing It is why
I touch you all I have is left is

sense of touch if I had my tongue
I would taste every part of your
body might taste like a tart wind
Tongue-less I touch you with my
fingertips as though to count
each hair on your body as though
to lift you up carefully slowly
tenderly Softly blowing like a
gentle tickling breeze you may
have thought of it I don't know
the edge of your chin your
fingertips unable to grope Was it
a tiny tornado or something like
it if only a wind had blown if only

a wind I would have stroked your
fragile drooping and dull hair if a
breeze had blown across this head
not mine my hesitating fingertips
my headless self as though nothing
was wrong if only a breeze had
blown from somewhere

*

How long has the tree
been holding you How
long have you been dying

Like a flower stem bent its
bud still dangling your
head's off hanging but still
holding on You're tied to
the tree like you're being
grafted on Looking at you
your head might be like a
blossom that hasn't dropped
Just like your head your body
may be struggling just barely
holding onto breath

I don't have a head so I must
be dead You do have a head so

you must be alive Can we say
that? I can move so I must be
alive I'm alive You can't move
so you must be dead Can we
say that? If I snip off your head
cut it clean off and stick it on
my body would life and death
switch places? Which side
would I be And you would you
be alive or dead as ever in a
daze compared to my head
whereabouts still unknown

But if you do are the

words coming out of
your mouth my words
or your words? Am I
seeing what your eyes see
or are you the one seeing?

I guess I won't recognize
it again your face No My
face No Your face No No
my your face forever

*

Everyone speaks

Everyone lives

though everyone dies

Is what decays

then melts

the body

or time?

Someone else closes their mouth

Chapter 3

Developing ***Beginning the End;***

Beginning the End. With him. At that time could he say he had his own will? Could I say that I had my own will? If the End had its own will it was towards death. The Beginning may be possible within premonition. Will premonition endure? And death. The Beginning tends towards the persistence of premonition. Endure and win. The End? The Beginning? What is left behind. Is it me? Is it him? At the End. The End. Will it end? The Beginning. Will it end? If it does Beginning the End. With him. The tangled up. Beginning. Of this concept. Ending. Beginning. The End. Again.

*

Developing ***Beginning the End;***

He lives his life. I live my life. The radii of our lives overlap at times. Delude ourselves there's overlap. In delusion. With him. The End. Beginning. Into an unknowable darkness. Hands stretch out. To grope. So that he doesn't even know he's him. Only with my sense of touch. Existing. Leaving be. He is sleeping. I don't wake him. Even if awake don't wake him. My fingertips. Within my radius. Existing. He is. He only sleeps. Ultimately never waking on my side.

Within the radius of my life. Eyes stay closed. With only my sense of touch. Existing. Leaving be. And failing. Always failing. Waiting. For him to wake. To not wake. To fail. My failure. His failure. Again. Waiting. Meeting. In failure. Meeting. Turning around. Always. Crossing paths. Cross. Ing. Again.

*

Developing ***Beginning the End;***

Rain falls. Rain stops. As if it never rained. He dies. He's dead. News of his death comes. His flesh. In life touched my flesh. That memory. Disappears with death. His flesh again. Comes to life in my flesh. Keeps living. He's dead. News of his death comes. Nothing. He only exists. In my flesh again. Rain falls. The trees like beasts. Become ferocious. Rain falls and stops. Coming? Going? He dies. He's dead. News of his death comes. His face. Quickly forgotten.

All night he. Draws one door. Stands in front of the door. With peeling paint. Door. Closed. Door. Blocked. From entering. Only stands in front of the door. Body drenched. Brr brr. Trembling. Rain doesn't. Come this evening. Matted hair. Sticks to a cold forehead. No one takes his hand through the door. No one pulls him in. Not outside the door. Only in front of the door. Only he. Is. Stupid inside the door. I'm not there. No one is outside the door. There is no door. No one says. Can't. He can't. Recognize me. Can't recognize me. Can't see me. Cannot.

He dies. Several times. He dies in my flesh. Like stains of rain. Spreads and permeates. Disappears from life. He into my flesh. Overflows. I suspect. My body is his. Rain falls in-between. The day clears up again. The day grows gloomy and the trees. Become ferocious and writhe. Bully and mix with each other. Trees become one forest. The wind blows through the forest. Shakes and sounds. Rain again. So much rain. The rain on my face. Falls in sweeps. He forgets. Me. Nothing. To him. He has no face. Again.

*

Developing ***Beginning the End;***

Beginning. With him. With a mother. With a dead. Child. With a nonexistent. Well. It appears. With the swamp. With dead. Poets. The End.

Again.

Part 3

Chapter 1

Y.o.u. s.t.o.p.

y.o.u. a.r.e. g.i.v.i.n.g. u.p. y.o.u.r. h.e.a.d.

When you're not touching you where are
you When you're not speaking to you
where are you When you're not touching
when you're not speaking are you and
your you wandering in a thick fog in
the land of the nonexistent With their
nothingness really when not touching
or when not speaking maybe there's too
much There's too much you and your you
crowding dense there's no difference
between them and the nonexistent Is

there one thing Is it existence and

nonexistence Is nonexistence nothing

L.e.a.n. a.g.a.i.n.s.t. t.h.e. t.r.e.e.

y.o.u.l.l. d.r.o.p. y.o.u.r. n.o.n.e.x.i.s.t.e.n.t. h.e.a.d.

A person was tied to the tree When he woke

his memory was a clean slate as though he

never had memories to begin with He was

naked His consciousness fading Barely

opening his eyes he saw no one was there

A swarm of faint light lingered around the

tree he was tied to Even faint light casts a

shadow his shadow and the tree's shadow

were one—sadly he didn't have the strength to lift his head and so his shadow was headless Even if he were to open his eyes even if the shadow were to open its eyes what use would it be Consciousness grows blurrier he barely grasps the tender thread of consciousness opening and closing his mouth over and over so much that not even his lips were visible And then the shadow begins to squirm something appears within the shadow The Thing stands the body upright little by little begins to crawl forward as he mumbles the Thing moves As if directing its movements to me he kept murmuring murmur move move

little by little minutely the Thing

approached him Approaches him

Y.o.u.r. h.a.n.d. f.a.l.l.s. w.e.a.k.l.y.

y.o.u.r. b.o.d.y. s.l.u.m.p.s. l.i.k.e. a. c.o.r.p.s.e.

I am that person The one calling the

Thing "you" The one calling you "you"

is me I named you into existence You

called me and I became you We are

both second person Even so you cannot

return to me and I cannot be certain

that I am the Thing borne from the

shadow Once created you don't

disappear easily You could say you

are the same before and after It's true

your ability to speak was unplanned

you break away from my oppression

with your words When you could spit

words you could speak for yourself

You are I I am you I am just you

S.i.l.e.n.c.e. c.r.a.w.l.s. u.p. y.o.u.

s.i.l.e.n.c.e. c.l.i.m.b.s. o.v.e.r. y.o.u.r. n.o.n.e.x.i.s.t.e.n.t. h.e.a.d.

What once was you moves no

longer It just slumps My
consciousness runs further
and further away somewhere
I can't hold onto gradually it
won't return We'll soon decay
I suppose Already the shadow
reeks of a foul odor rots away
Within whose voice will I
decay Within whose words
will I emerge be bound then
vanish But who is it that keeps
talking to me goading me Who
is the person before the question
who is the person after the

question Who stuffed me in the

middle of this question can't they

stop this who keeps listening

to me speak to the bitter end

T.h.e. s.i.l.e.n.c.e.

o.n.l.y. s.i.l.e.n.c.e.

The voice is fading away

I don't think I can return

to this place again

Where are you when not touching

where am I when not speaking

Where are we Are you

gone so where are you

Where are you in time?

Chapter 2

That's what it is The explanation that's what it is You've already ceased to move you no longer speak through those words within those words I moved but now my movements have stopped Somehow it seemed trees I cannot see encircled me You see it seems as though this is a place I've been before I don't even know if this is a tree I'm leaning on If it is it feels like there are many more trees apart from this tree around us watching us This body is just a body but what I'm saying is what I'm saying from this body mayhap this is a forest

You too must already know this well This forest when night falls the wind blows and the trees growl like beasts When night falls the trees open their nonexistent eyelids a gaze not there like will-o'-the-wisp glares wildly bares its nonexistent blood-stained teeth Sound wandered here preexisted the trees the branches raised up the forest When night falls neighboring trees and my body face each other Unknowable tears fell leaving behind gouges on this tree and that tree On that tree this tree's gouge was so defined the entire forest shakes It's that kind of forest

Each tree has a trace of the carnivorous it's that kind of forest It may be that I was bested by the trees who knows My head was mayhap eaten by the trees and thrown into darkness flat and unable to discern from ground and flesh It may be that I am the already dead child of the nonexistent mother who knows Snow from a nonexistent well and though never birthed I may be the child who drowned in the swamp Head eaten up by carnivorous trees the nonexistent mother the nonexistent well the child never birthed but drowned in the swamp I may be the protagonist of this nonsense perhaps mayhap perhaps

That's what it is The explanation that's what it is A little while ago when I screamed Hey! Is there anyone out there? What I didn't hear was your response Even though I named you "you" I've never heard you speak I've only called you "you" why have you ignored me your listener The question makes my absent head throb Sigh I grow lonesome The fact that the words of someone I used to touch don't come to me lends a chill to this place gloomy and goosebumps sprout sprout on flesh It was fine when I had no personal pronoun I could be someone anyone Mayhap I didn't like it Even so this is so

But if I at last was borne out of words within your shadow and rose Then that must mean my words live within your words But if your words have already stopped What I'm saying is who does this bizarre hoarse voice belong to? You your flesh is already festering and my body is returning to it Apart from your barebone voice your words my words within your words all of it is pushed into silence I mean I'm faintly faintly forgetting if there were ever words here to begin with Are you here to hear these fading words You must be here listening in order to forget

Perhaps this place is in Oblivion Somehow you are breaking apart and piecing together shards of Oblivion's landscape Somehow this may be the before of anyone's someone's everyone's swallowed silence It could be the after-speech the before and after that arises from words Somehow this voice says the Thing wakes the voice this voice could be someone's delusion layer upon layer a landscape appearing—no not appearing One moment—no one season—no about a thousand years You and I and your movement and touch words spilling out disappearing forgetting within silence At long last rumors that we were gone the forest forms sways the nonexistent mother appears the dead child emerges the nonexistent well becomes an overgrown swamp

Chapter 3

Darkness recedes

The day grows light

again Sunlight

streams in through

the window It's not

yesterday's light

The noise outside

the window is also

not the noise of

yesterday I clutched

the letters of yesterday

those words became

precarious once more

layering on all night

Beginning the End

already ***With him***

the sunlight gnaws in

the middle of nibbling

Beginning the End has

gone out into the world

fleeing the sunlight

floating around the

room avoiding ever

being captured again

I'm at risk trying to

excavate today's letters

writing and unable to

write when I think of

me I am me letters

keep butting in-between

I keep trying to break

free from me Not me

even if not I keep

cutting in reflecting

like sunlight On the

contrary even if noisy

the letters spill out

from the windows

yet don't overflow Full

of outings I can't see

the letters There are

too many of them

it's impossible to name

each one on an outing

nameless and floating

about only looking

blanky at ***Beginning***

the End gnawinggnawing

floating and vacantly

over and over inside

the room I'm writing

and I can't write this

again and again

Yesterday's me then

today's outing called

for in the middle of it

one thing was chosen
switching bodies after
switching I rushed to
hide in-between letters
and couldn't tell them
apart not knowing their
names not having
named them unknowing
if I am me just like me
Already useless I am
writing and unable to
write Before I get any
bigger before I lose
my breath before I

write before I can't

write trying to go back

but trying not to go

devoured ***with***

Only crumbs leftover

he is all that's left

stolen from the sunlight

grasping and Barely

opening the door to

outside Outside snow

falling furiously with no

sunlight Across the

snow flurries the

neighbors with bleak

eyes shine And don't
show the end or the
beginning he is also
there a voice white
If you locked eyes
only then would
words whiter than
snow come unstuck
from the mouth to
soon melt away words
(A thing wakes
in darkness)
Words whiter
than snow erasing

the gaze erasing the
neighbors erasing me
spilling returning
to the room unable
to find the way back
Tail bitten by tail
cutting off this
allegory's tail
unable to find a
method to end this
Before the neighbors
catch on hurriedly
catching my voice
hiding in the snow

in the snowfall Into
the snowstorm Going
still going going

Epilogue

After the beast went away he was
engrossed in the words left behind
He gathered up all the meanings
that its words could possibly hold
in the end he left for home without
applying meaning to his words
Departure returning or leaving a
place that one returns to what else
could that be but home he thought
Meanings without words wore down
faded crumbled Only traces of the
beast linger throughout the house
Though it may not be an orangutan
it could be called an orangutan He

found in old literature that the beast
knows human speech but can't
escape its beastly past He couldn't
uncover whether the beast could
become human if it could break free
And so from the fragments of the
traces the beast left behind a wan
me was born I couldn't see but I
was pallid and had no voice In the
beginning he lent me his voice
however his voice was too hoarse
It was bizarre beyond measure
I abandoned him in order to find a
different voice I left his home Like

meanings I too thought I'd fall apart
I became a voice collector I would
choose days especially bleak when
the weather looked as though it
would pour at any moment snow or
rain I wandered the streets On those
days on street corners in the dark
corners there's usually someone
crouched there I never once just
passed them by hastily—so they
didn't catch on—I stole their voice
and hung it around my neck Wearing
a necklace of voices trilling roaring
the voices trembled From the voices

I had my choice of my voice
Occasionally passing alleyways there
were lucky days I'd gain a voice
drifting over walls I would examine
each one meticulously A voice too
sad or too depressed is prone to
spoiling instantly when a rage-filled
voice crosses over the wall and clings
you must be very careful The voice's
unkempt owner will give chase If you
don't flee at once your other voices
are at risk of being stolen from you
Though the beast does its best to
speak like humans it can't escape

its beast identity its voice retains a
trace of beastliness Somehow I feel
like you must be the owner of that
voice When will it be where will it
be I don't know in a bit I think you
and I will come upon each other
And then don't be too flustered you
won't notice until the next day you'll
realize that your voice has disappeared
Just a moment before I came across
someone like you underneath the
creepy telephone pole I'm on my
way back from lifting a voice In fact
this place is growing old and the

future will wear out and even these
sentences will soon crumble and fall
apart that may be why I'm searching
for your voice immediately no matter
what your voice says that's the truth
it is nothing Your throat gibbers
away with words that mean nothing
yet I want to take the voices hanging
around my throat and drape them
around yours Who knows maybe then
a rosy smile will frame my pallid face
maybe it will spread It's time to begin
the end I murmur in someone else's
voice now it's your turn Though you

haven't started yet it seems your words
it seems your laughter won't end I'm a
voice collector Even today I wander the
streets searching for your voice Are
you there? If you're there hurry
and find me Hurry and know me

Enough

Be the master of my voices

POET'S NOTE

I have written a long poem for the first time. The decision to write it was made about five years earlier, motivated by a man who awakened from his slumbers in darkness. Upon waking, the man scribbled something on many sheets of paper. I had no idea of what would become of him or, if he had awakened to tell me something, what on earth it was. I kept those sheets in a file and carried them around. The edges of the sheets became frayed. Every now and then, I would look at the scribbles, but I always avoided him, trying to run away from him time and again. In the meantime, I got my new poems published. I must admit, though, I owed some of the ideas in them to the images emerged while he was being scribbled. I cannot say for certain that his appearance was the turning point, but I knew that my poems were stepping into another, unfamiliar world of Language.

Last winter, I finally made a conscious effort

to bring the man into my poetry; even then, I knew nothing about him. It was sheer luck that I found the expression "***Beginning the End***" in my notebook. Writing the mysterious man, I hung onto the expression. I was still none the wiser about what he intended to signify, or why "***Beginning the End***" had to be the title of the poem. Hence, the loquacity, speculation, and incoherency in this poem originated from not knowing. The whole process of writing this poem was in itself a journey towards knowing, which, as you know, is bound to fail. I expect, however, the failure to be the beginning of a new language.

The production of this poem was riddled with resurging moments of excitement, despair, doubts and delays. In the midst of it all, though, I tried hard, to the end, not to stray from such concepts of writing as contingency and improvisation. Perhaps, the poem still needs more contingencies and improvisations. But this is the limit of my ability. Even if the limit already lay in store for me from the moment the man awakened in the dark, I have no choice but to love it. It may be the limit of my language and at the same time, that of the world that I am situated in. After having fallen desperately in love, I will be ready to cross over again. In that new sphere of creation, I believe, I will try to construct yet another exciting world of Language where loquacity, speculation, incoherency, or perhaps some other things germinate and grow to the full. I also believe that such attempts of mine may end up in failure.

THE POET'S ESSAY

K
POET

Speaking of Ruins (*Pyeheo*),

1.

May I ask you where you are? I can only answer I am in the ruins. If I ask you where you live? Then, I can't only answer I live in the ruins. Are all places ruins? Only, ruins, let's just say. Are you there? Uttering the plosive *pye*, I feel something slipping out from my body. Is the body a place? With my lips still open, I pronounce *heo*. Now, I feel more, more, and more of that something leaving my body, even though there is nothing left to leave. Is the body time? Nothing remains. What was there? Nothing. If there was nothing whatsoever, what then could have slipped out? There was, if nothing else, the fact that nothing was there. You mean, absence?

The fact that there was something is inherent in the fact that there was nothing. Is it time? Time is placed in sentences. Is it the wind? Yes, it is the wind. Is it traces? It is remains. May I ask if you are alive? I just am. *Pyeheo* just is. It has not yet disappeared. Are you sure it is you? What else but ruins?

2.

Did you go?

No, I couldn't. When Poet Leon showed me the picture, I felt as if I was crumbling down little by little into the picture. As if being worn away. Against the background of a dazzlingly blue sky, beautiful curves of the sand dunes were floating around in the picture. And there vividly emerged the remains of buildings half buried in the Mexican desert sand dunes. The village had been hit by a sandstorm, I was told. It was curious. But we had to cancel our scheduled visit to the village because another poet invited us to lunch. It was difficult to turn down the invitation since it was a special arrangement to welcome us poets who had come all the way from the opposite side of the earth. The lunch lasted for six hours. The chef kept bringing out new dishes from the backyard. For six hours, we ate the foods and drank tequila and mescal. It was fun and strange at the same time. What if we had gone to the desert? If I had gone to see the ruins, would I be able to bring to my mind more striking images of the ruins?

Did you go?

No, I couldn't. And yet I had written a poem about a desert. In the poem, the desert is a faraway place harboring someone unreachable. Perhaps, it was impossible to reach the desert. Later, I even tried to depict the city where I live as a ruin, overlapping it with those desert images. Come to think of it, I might have already foreseen through my poems the photo Leon showed me. If the desert is a timeless place, the ruins still keep the real time in themselves. The photo Leon showed me and the poems that I wrote long ago, I think, all show the sight of atemporality eating into the real time. Deserts belong to a completely different temporality. Outside. Unimaginable. Even our imagination, perhaps, wears off and assimilates into the colossal nothingness.

Did you go?

I said I couldn't. Speaking of which, I am obsessed with ruins. Obsessed with the image of time before it is completely buried under the desert. Ruins also most certainly belong to a different temporality. The instant a place begins to turn into ruins, it starts to run away from the real time that it has accumulated. While it is on the run, the time that has yet to come replaces the real time, or so it seems. We get to watch oblivion transforming, slowly but more steadily than we think it would, memories and bodies. In a daze. Oblivion lays down in front of us a load of mysterious time. At the ruins, we come face to face with, not the transience of man and the world that belong to the real time, but an unfamiliar, unprecedented face of time making an unexpected appearance. It stirs within us a sense of foreboding that the unfamiliarity will little by little corrode and wear down the present time, starting from its very foundation. If not, why would I be obsessed with ruins?

You went there, didn't you?

Yes, I did, but I would rather say I discovered than I went. No, wait a minute. Am I the one that was discovered? I am still confused whether that place discovered me or I discovered that place. As I told you before, the reservoir in my hometown, I mean the village submerged under that reservoir water. The summer I turned eighteen, I was wandering around in the reservoir bed after the water had drained.

Only then did the sight of the ruins jumped out at me. As a matter of fact, I had known it all along, but at that very moment, I rediscovered them. That village was involved in the partisan activities that went on even after the war. A panic-stricken rumor had it that after the partisans were subjugated, they blocked the reservoir on purpose to sink the village under water. Even a rumor of a tiger, though never seen, was also prowling around. Understandable, since there was a mountain peak named Tiger Peak. Above all, it was my father's and grandfather's birthplace. Now, under the water is their hometown.

You went there, didn't you?

I will never go back there. In fact, I cannot. Not anymore. The name of the village that emerged from the drained reservoir, having devoured the name of its neighboring village on the higher ground, pretended to be the original village. That is where I was born. As a result, my father, my grandfather, and I have the same birthplace in name, but different ones in place. Weird. The house I was born in got buried under the ground when an expressway was constructed. Now, my birthplace is under a heap of earth. Countless absences beyond memories that set out from the ruins and are being born, only born, endlessly, one after another—uncanny. I have long believed that my poems are born of those absences that slither on and on like a snake even after escaping the ruins. What then, made me go there and discover the place? I wonder if the ruins had discovered me, I mean, if the ruins had chosen me. I, as an eighteen-year-old boy, was just walking, when the monsoon rains temporarily let up, towards the red light waving on the far side of the reservoir, simply walking towards it, that was all, nothing else, I swear. Perhaps that is when the ruins possessed my body. And over a few decades since, they used my body as their host, living inside me like parasites, and eating into me to increase their size. And now, they finally dominate my entire existence, that's what I think. Why else would I be so obsessed with ruins?

3.

All the faith that supported me has collapsed. Is it the interior? It is the world. Inconsistencies are prevalent like viruses. Is it an exaggeration? It is the present reality. How is it? The poor, foolish thing is still breathing. Dying out? It merely ekes out, holding onto few remaining pillars of its values. Downfall? I would say: Nevertheless. Some hopes, perhaps? It gives out a terrible stench! Is it a mixture of both? It is in-between already and not quite yet. Times that fail to belong to either become ruins. Endlessly propagating themselves and infecting others. You mean time? I mean chaos. Will it arrive? Sadness will. Are you certain? My answer is: We were dead and were able to breathe.[*] Will it emerge? It will disperse. In the end. I too. The world too. Is another, different time being created anew somewhere? Being born anew somewhere? Language. Will it come alive? It is the ruins.

* Paul Celan "Memory of France"

COMMENTARY

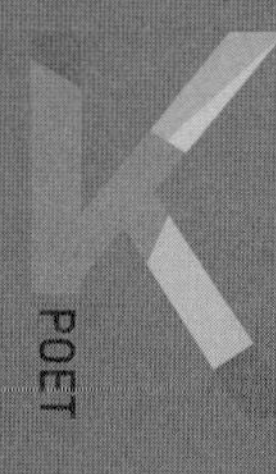

Writing and Speaking Born of Oblivion

Kim Tae-seon(Critic)

0.

When the sun sets and dusk falls, a man writes 'Beginning the End.' Having watched the sunlight eating away all day long the letters on the old bookshelves, he wonders if the leftover letters would fall prey to darkness now. He could be foreseeing, in the disappearance of letters, the end of a certain time, which is on its way towards him. 'Beginning the End,' according to him, means the progress "Beyond faded and worn splintering crumbling right before it disappears." By willingly taking part in the progression towards disappearance, he attempts to use it as the source of his capacity. His writing 'Beginning the End' may be an expression of his will to control the gargantuan passivity to which all things are destined to submit.

However, it seems impossible to use death as a source of capacity to write. The impossibility notwithstanding, the phrase 'Beginning the End' stubornly clings to him like Spanish needles and urges him to keep writing. One day, he discovered his own old expression in the incomprehensible words of an animal that came to him as if it were an afflatus. Ever since the day, he has been possessed with writing. Anxiously watching all the letters inside himself disappearing, he endeavors to catch hold of the remaining letters, hoping to complete his work with their help. The story we encounter while reading his anthology *Beginning the End* is about the curious shifts from germination to extinction to transition accomplished by a certain kind of speaking, which can be experienced in the process of writing. Nevertheless, these movements or shifts are shrouded in darkness, so it is impossible to articulate them. Thus, the poet's job is to stay with darkness, moving from darkness to darkness.

1.

'It' awakens in the dark. 'I' says, "*Just the fact of its consciousness makes me speak*." Here, we come face to face with a contradiction intrinsic in writing or speaking. That is, the curious paradox that "*the event of its awakening emerges I begin to speak*," but at the same time, what enables 'I' to speak is 'the fact that It awakens.' Before speaking, 'It' has not yet awoken. And without 'Its' awakening, there can be no speaking. All the difficulties of writing originate from the impossibility of beginning like this. Nonetheless, 'I' starts speaking, pushing through the impossibility. What makes speaking possible here is not 'I' but the existence of 'It' that has been awakened not only by speaking but also along with speaking.

The identity of 'It' is hidden in the dark. In the first chapter of Part 1, the narrator makes a premise that 'It' is a person; otherwise, 'I's' speaking cannot reach 'It.' As speaking continues, 'Its' body becomes shaped and even capable of moving, and yet 'I's' speaking does not get any clearer. Moreover, 'I' seems to focus on and apprehend nothing else but the moment of 'Its' birth. As is detectible in the questions "How far can words move Words can't be unraveled they hesitate and linger how deeply can they stagnate?" 'I' does not have speaking under his control.

"Hey! Is there anyone out there?" begins the second chapter, a question asked by the being that is called 'It' in the first chapter. The question is not answered. Further, although 'It' is said to have started speaking, 'Its' speech remains to be nothing more than some sounds that have yet to become speaking. And yet, 'It' states, "until I can speak I'll keep trickling sound that's my plan." 'It' touches his own body with fingertips and tells us about the tactile experience in which he acquires senses and feels the world around him expanding: "My body is being molded." Meanwhile, 'It' realizes that he cannot recognize himself and asks, "why am I calling myself me" Calling onesclf 'I' requires the existence of the other. The signs uttered by 'I' should be responded by the other, and the response should also be received by 'I.'

As 'It' questions about his instance as an 'I,' 'It' also discovers that he cannot touch his own head. Perhaps, the absence of the head is the reason 'Its' utterances remain some sounds that have yet to become speaking. It may also imply the fact that 'It' cannot govern 'Its' self. As soon as 'It' realizes he is headless, he imagines his limbs "shakes aimlessly" and his body moving arbitrarily; 'It' also experiences his body suffers a case of terrible lethargy, unable to move properly. Soon, it occurs to 'It' that he may be devoured by and decay in the darkness. Here, 'Its' disorientation and lethargy are on the same trajectory as 'I's' unsuccessful speaking in the first chapter.

In the third chapter, the narrator is a person who intends to write. He first writes '*Beginning the End*' and then opens the story with "I wanted to write Even as I saw myself." He wishes to write about the trees with carnivorous traces, the emergence of a swamp where a child has drowned, the noises of gulping down something, "The sounds of eating devouring annihilation and creation," "A silent mother Countlessmothers who don't exist keep getting up

Get up and beat me endlessly," etc., but the phrase 'Beginning the End' wedges itself in between these images time and again. In the end, what he wished to write remains unwritten. Saying, "now in a room that's wearing down the black of my body tends to leak into darkness," he feels that all of his capacity to write has drained away. Even with his capacity exhausted, even while thinking whatever he does will only end up fading and wearing out, he still writes 'Beginning the End.' What would it mean to keep writing when there is absolutely no hope left?

2.

In the first chapter of Part 2, 'It' is now called 'You.' The second person is used, according to the narrator, because of the premise of 'It' being a person. But then he brings forward another, more revealing reason: The 'I'-'You' division somehow makes 'I' feel that he has the authority to allow You to be here and to give directions to You with no interference from anyone else. 'I's' directing 'You' is also a way of governing his own speaking. The reason for the headlessness of 'It,' who is now called 'You,' is given as well. 'You' cannot see 'I' and further, 'You' cannot have any thoughts of his own. 'I' wants to keep 'You' completely under his control: "if you can see me and think about me that's not complete oppression." The strategy of separation and subordination may well be the wish of those who intend to keep the act of writing under the complete control of their capacities and designs. However, it is a false hope to have an absolute power over the act of writing. Writing, or speaking for that matter, will never follow 'I's' designs, nor move only under 'I's' government. Once words, either written or spoken, get separated out from 'I's' body, they have their own lives outside 'I's' reign.

Now, let's watch 'You' (previously 'It') meeting a

body tied to a tree. 'You' begins to grope the body with fingertips, slowly from the feet upwards. Until this moment, 'You' seems to faithfully follow the instructions given in 'I's' speaking. But when the fingertips reach the chin past the Adam's apple of the body tied to the tree, 'I' blurts out, "*I should stop speaking*." As evinced in "*The words that bound you grab me by the throat From my constricted throat words seep out like air from a deflating balloon*," speaking has become 'I's' fetter. 'I' would like to stop speaking, but the being that has awakened along with speaking will not allow it.

In the second chapter, 'You' (previously 'It') begins to speak. 'You' calls the body tied to the tree 'Ja-ne' (meaning 'you,' informal). 'You' and 'Ja-ne' appear to be in contradiction with, almost antipodal to each other. 'You' can move but has no head; 'Ja-ne' has a head but tied to the tree, unable to move. 'You' stays awake and utters sounds, but 'Ja-ne,' even with a mouth to speak and ears to hear with, is not awake, therefore unable to speak or hear. Even after meeting the other being, 'You' fails to get the solutions to his speaking problems from him. That never deters, though, 'You' from making attempts to speak. 'You' wonders if 'Ja-ne's' head is removed and put on his shoulders, "would life and death switch places?" If that happened, 'You' continues: Who would be on the life's side and who on the death's side? The words coming out of the mouth, whose words would they be? Although unsuccessful in getting the answers to his questions, 'It' comes to realize that regardless of the answers, one would be able to speak and the other would end up shutting his mouth.

In the third chapter, there is 'an attempt to develop the theme of *Beginning the End*.' Unlike in Part 1, after the expression 'Beginning the End' comes 'together with He.' In this chapter, though, the person called ‘He’ is not clearly identified and simply depicted as a person who dies repeatedly. “He lives his life. I live my life. The radii of our lives overlap at times. Delude ourselves there's overlap.” Although remaining anonymous, ‘He’ must be, be it an existing person or a conceptual being created by speaking, someone who has influenced ‘I's’ writing to a certain extent; or, their writings must have interacted with each other.

“Beginning the End. With him.” This expression and the motif of repetition go hand in hand. “He dies. Several times. He dies in my flesh. Like stains of rain. Spreads and permeates. Disappears from life. He into my flesh. Overflows.” Although the speaking is interrupted by so many periods, it is to begin ‘again’ in case the writing ends up unsuccessful; in other words, the periods or interruptions are at once trials and errors made while attempting ‘Beginning the End.’ The stories intermittently arranged in the third chapter are the reappearing fragments of those that have once reached oblivion. Writers try to translate these fragments into Language. However, in order to speak together with those that have been to oblivion, writing should also move towards the capacity to erase itself, that is, to get on the path leading to a perfect silence through repetition.

3.

In the first chapter of Part 3, 'You' (previously 'It') stops moving and the man tied to the tree awakes. His consciousness is getting clouded. Try as he might to keep his eyes open, all he can make out is his own shadow on the floor cast by dim light. He cannot lift his head and even his shadow is headless. But then when he moves his lips, the shadow suddenly stirs, raises itself and starts crawling towards him. That's it. His shadow is nothing but 'It' that was born together with speaking. Here, the secret of speaking is revealed. 'You,' the being called 'Ja-ne,' and 'I' are one and the same. Moreover, as 'I's' speaking makes 'It' 'You,' 'You's' speaking also makes 'I' 'Ja-ne.' In Part 1 and 2, speaking may appear to be a lonely act that takes place in isolation. However, 'I's' act of speaking, as a matter of fact, always creates 'You,' even if 'You' is just a potential being.

Interestingly, the narrator in the first chapter asks where 'You' and 'You's' 'Ja-ne' are when he himself is not speaking. When speaking stops, are those born along with speaking "wandering in a thick fog in the land of the nonexistent." At this point, we should pay attention to the truth that 'nonexistents' do not disappear into a vacuum nothingness, but do exist as 'nonexistents' in and of themselves. When speaking shifts to silence, things to be spoken of and those already spoken of are not simply erased to be part of the state of vacuum, but perhaps transport themselves into a certain realm of potentiality. However, mortal beings, faced with a shift towards disappearance, feel anxiety produced by the fear of death or the unknown. Watching 'It' that used to be 'You' turning motionless, 'I' asks: "Within whose voice will I decay?"

Speaking is a process of temporary existence. While speaking, 'I' experiences continuous disappearance. 'I's' instinct to preserve his existence would have him perceive from the experience a gloomy future prospect. Nevertheless, speaking presented in the form of questions never stops. It is because of You who are listening carefully to my speaking. However, You keep silent to the end and 'I' realizes his own voice is disappearing and he will never be able to return to this place. Does reaching silence mean the speaking 'I' stops existing as well? When speaking comes to a halt, 'You,' to whom 'I's' speaking is directed, would be at 'when'?

In the second chapter of Part 3, 'It' is still speaking. 'It' is speaking in the wood where trees with carnivorous traces grow and the fragments of oblivion haunt, about which the narrator in the third chapter of Part 1 intended to write. "Perhaps this place is in Oblivion Somehow you are breaking apart and piecing together shards of Oblivion's landscape." The wood is therefore the realm of oblivion where a being of Language arrives when speaking stops. In other words, it is before and after speaking. In this realm, "one season—no about a thousand years You and I and your movement and touch words spilling out disappearing forgetting within silence At long last rumors that we were gone the forest forms sways the nonexistent mother appears the dead child emerges the nonexistent well becomes an overgrown swamp" come to settle.

Generally speaking, oblivion means the disappearance of memory or the loss of memory. However, there is another kind of oblivion. That is the movement of oblivion called 'bold oblivion' by Martin Heidegger in his analysis of Hölderlin's poetics. It is a movement leading to the realm of the essence, which remains hidden in reality. To accomplish the goal of 'bold oblivion,' an effort to go beyond 'I' or to erase 'I,' in other words, to break away from self-obsession is necessary. The narrator in the third chapter speaks of his experience of writing: "when I think of/me I am me letters/keep butting in-between/I keep trying to break/free from me Not me." Even after this experience, however, 'I' still intervenes over and over, making writing impossible. In order to gain freedom from 'I,' 'I' tries to erase 'I' and carry out the march towards oblivion 'together with He.' Perhaps, 'Beginning the End' is an effort made by 'I' accompanied by 'He,' to achieve selfless writing or writing born of the 'bold oblivion.'

0.

From the Prologue to Part 3, the one who is engaged in the act of speaking and writing is 'I,' but in the Epilogue, 'I' has become 'He.' The speaking voice in the Epilogue is 'It' the speaking being that was born with speaking. 'I' has been erased and now 'It' speaks of his own volition. 'It' abandons 'I's', i.e., 'He's' voice and becomes a collector of other voices. Any work, once it leaves the writer's hand, erases the existence of the writer and begins to put on the reader's voice. The work conveys its emotions to the reader who in turn becomes transformed. The reader himself, while reading the work, changes the voice of the work. While interacting like this, they lose their existing shapes and change into something else. Beyond the isolated instance called 'I,' the repetitive process of pushing through oblivion takes place not only during the process of speaking and writing but also during that of listening and reading.

After the processes of listening and reading are all over, even after 'I's' speaking stops at the end of the story, 'You' the reader will undergo another process of oblivion, carrying on the process of speaking indefinitely in a rich variety of fashions. The reading experience, even when it has gone to the other side of oblivion and no longer remains in consciousness, even inside the unconscious, keeps conversing with the other experiences and at times influences the reader's life in one way or another. 'To Begin the End' is to participate in the oblivion's march during which the self is erased. Through the march, the lives of those, who have considered themselves as isolated individuals, begin overlap with one another; and that is when an exceptional event called 'dialogue' occurs. "I wander the/streets searching for your voice Are/you there? If you're there hurry/and find me Hurry and know me//

Enough//Be the master of my voices." 'Beginning the End End' is also 'I's' opening up himself to you, hoping to hear your voice. It is an invitation to never-ending dialogues.

WHAT THEY SAY ABOUT KIM KEUN

Kim Keun brings his unique metaphors and original rhythms into poetry not to immediately relieve the ever-mounting, unbearable poetic tension, but to give birth to poetry that gets conceived through constant interactions with others. To accomplish this goal, he equips himself with an indomitable willpower and resilience, and wages war against the world, himself, the others, and the conventions. Refusing to settle for the status quo, he makes a critical decision to break away from the blind belief in the formalist aesthetics and the content-centered poetics possessed with absurd notions. And he resolutely draws out from within himself the communal poetry, the poetry that is constantly reviewed and self-reviewing, the poetry originating from the strong will and felt necessity to hold together, in the name of community, the constantly dispersing poetic consciousness.

Cho Chae-ryong, "Community' s Projet to Search for the Missing Nephew—On the Courage for the Transition of

Poetics", *Han'guk Munhak*, 2013.

Kim Keun the poet, in his first anthology Snake-Boy's Outing, narrates his painful journey through the amorphous, elusive fictional chronotope, which he has taken in order to put into action his hope for "there, not here," his longing for the "outside, not the inside," in other words, to break away from the space he was fenced in. But then again, in his second anthology Meet You at the Cloud Theater, he is still searching for the space granted to those like himself whose long-endeavored but repeatedly failed attempts to abandon the inside to join the outside have made it impossible for them even to return to the inside. Kim Keun then comes to realize that those who are lost are allowed to remain only in spaces amorphous like clouds, unreal like projected screens. Nevertheless, the poet still fathoms the possibility of 'our' encounters even in those spaces.

He smiles at both life and death. A poet's individuality consists of his own paradoxes or ironies to which Kim Keun himself unexceptionally owes his uniqueness. Now he seems more ready than ever to understand life through reflecting upon death and embrace death as part of life. While mixing his body with those of the people who are possessed or have burning bodies or 'eyes for the sole purpose of crying,' he has transformed himself into an eternally uninflammable eye (i.e., book) and begun to unflinchingly face up to the world. He seems resolute in his belief that it is the poet's solemn task to record the screams (bimyong)[*] of those who have met an untimely death (bimyong)[**] in their epitaphs (bimyong)[***]. Granting that it is not the only right path, it is one of the most painful and yet most honorable

* 嗚 (비명): 'scream' pronounced bimyong

** 非命 (비명): 'untimely death' pronounced bimyong

*** 碑銘 (비명): 'epitaph' pronounced bimyong [*,**,*** are homonyms] paths for a poet to take. Those who are on this path. How many of them are there? There is only one Kim Keun among the poets who were born in the 1970s and started out in the 2000s.

Shin Hyoung-Chol, *The collapse of the Ethica*, 2008.

※ 'Poet' s Note' 'The Poet' s Essay' 'Commentary' 'What They Say About Kim Keun'

Translated by Jeon Miseli

K-POET
Beginning the End

Written by Kim Keun
Translated by Deborah Kim
Published by ASIA Publishers
Address 445, Hoedong-gil, Paju-si, Gyeonggi-do, Korea
Tel (8231).955.7958
Fax (8231).955.7956
Email bookasia@hanmail.net
Homepage Address www.bookasia.org

ISBN 979-11-5662-317-5 (set) | 979-11-5662-566-7(04810)

First published in Korea by ASIA Publishers 2021

This book is published with the support of the Literature Translation Institute of Korea (LTI Korea).

K-픽션 한국 젊은 소설

최근에 발표된 단편소설 중 가장 우수하고 흥미로운 작품을 엄선하여 출간하는 〈K-픽션〉은 한국문학의 생생한 현장을 국내외 독자들과 실시간으로 공유하고자 기획되었습니다. 원작의 재미와 품격을 최대한 살린 〈K-픽션〉 시리즈는 매 계절마다 새로운 작품을 선보입니다.

001 버핏과의 저녁 식사-**박민규** Dinner with Buffett-**Park Min-gyu**
002 아르판-**박형서** Arpan-**Park hyoung su**
003 애드벌룬-**손보미** Hot Air Balloon-**Son Bo-mi**
004 나의 클린트 이스트우드-**오한기** My Clint Eastwood-**Oh Han-ki**
005 이베리아의 전갈-**최민우** Dishonored-**Choi Min-woo**
006 양의 미래-**황정은** Kong's Garden-**Hwang Jung-eun**
007 대니-**윤이형** Danny-**Yun I-hyeong**
008 퇴근-**천명관** Homecoming-**Cheon Myeong-kwan**
009 옥화-**금희** Ok-hwa-**Geum Hee**
010 시차-**백수린** Time Difference-**Baik Sou linne**
011 올드 맨 리버-**이장욱** Old Man River-**Lee Jang-wook**
012 권순찬과 착한 사람들-**이기호** Kwon Sun-chan and Nice People-**Lee Ki-ho**
013 알바생 자르기-**장강명** Fired-**Chang Kangmyoung**
014 어디로 가고 싶으신가요-**김애란** Where Would You Like To Go?-**Kim Ae-ran**
015 세상에서 가장 비싼 소설-**김민정** The World's Most Expensive Novel-**Kim Min-jung**
016 체스의 모든 것-**김금희** Everything About Chess-**Kim Keum-hee**
017 할로윈-**정한아** Halloween-**Chung Han-ah**
018 그 여름-**최은영** The Summer-**Choi Eunyoung**
019 어느 피씨주의자의 종생기-**구병모** The Story of P.C.-**Gu Byeong-mo**
020 모르는 영역-**권여선** An Unknown Realm-**Kwon Yeo-sun**
021 4월의 눈-**손원평** April Snow-**Sohn Won-pyung**
022 서우-**강화길** Seo-u-**Kang Hwa-gil**
023 가출-**조남주** Run Away-**Cho Nam-joo**
024 연애의 감정학-**백영옥** How to Break Up Like a Winner-**Baek Young-ok**
025 창모-**우다영** Chang-mo-**Woo Da-young**
026 검은 방-**정지아** The Black Room-**Jeong Ji-a**
027 도쿄의 마야-**장류진** Maya in Tokyo-**Jang Ryu-jin**
028 홀리데이 홈-**편혜영** Holiday Home-**Pyun Hye-young**
029 해피 투게더-**서장원** Happy Together-**Seo Jang-won**
030 골드러시-**서수진** Gold Rush-**Seo Su-jin**